Chandra,

Happy Birthday!
We miss you ♡
Austin misses you!

Love,
      Jamie

HAIKU AUSTIN

love song to Austin
in 17 syllables
wonderful and weird

CARLOTTA EIKE STANKIEWICZ

HAIKU
EMPIRE
PRESS

Haiku Austin
Copyright ©2016 by Carlotta Eike Stankiewicz

Published by Haiku Empire Press in Austin, Texas

Inquiries:
info@haikuAustin.com

FIRST EDITION

First Printing May 2016

Cataloging-in-Publication Data
Stankiewicz, Carlotta Eike
Haiku Austin

p.   cm.

1. Poetry 2. Haiku - poetry
3. Austin Texas poetry 4. Austin Texas photographs
I. Carlotta Eike Stankiewicz II. Haiku Austin
ISBN 978-0-9974770-0-9   Pbk
2016906291

All photographs by Carlotta Eike Stankiewicz
Book design by Anne Stevenson

Printed in the United States of America
at OneTouchPoint-Southwest in Austin, Texas

dedicated to
  my favorite Austinites
Kate and Ella S

Welcome to HaikuAustin

If you've picked this book up, I'm guessing you get it. Whether you've spent a weekend, a week, a year or a lifetime here, there's something about Austin that calls to you. I felt it when I first visited, 24 years ago, and knew instantly that I'd come home. Austin's been good to me, and I wanted to return the favor. As someone who loves playing with words as much as I love capturing moments with my camera, I knew the combination of poetry and photography was the only way to pay tribute. This is my offering to Austin...and to you.

Iconic Austin

how to define it?
Texas meets weird meets awesome
yeah, that's my Austin

Alamo Drafthouse to Zilker Park, this city has lots to love,
y'all. Topping the list are those indelible icons that will
forever hold a special place in your heart and your daydreams,
whether you've been here 20 years or 20 minutes.

The Paramount
star of Congress Ave
  her bright lights and balconies
put on a good show

Size Matters
dwarfing D.C.'s dome
  everything's bigger here
this is Texas, y'all

At the Capitol
even in winter
  politics as usual
means a lot of hot air

Moonlight Towers
halos in the sky
    blessing Austin with their glow
tempting teens to climb

Monumental
that erect red sign
   so close and yet so far out
obscenely perfect

Lucy in Disguise
sequins and Spandex
drag queens flirt with evil clowns
grown-ups play dress-up

Zilker Christmas tree
lights turned into tree
   tower over Zilker Park
let's go for a spin

Zilker Zephyr
tiny shiny train
   cramped parents, filled with wonder
"When can we get off?"

Mount Bonnell
the best perch in town
    to admire Lake Austin and
look down on the rich

The Driskill
handsome and haunted
    tourists, hipsters, dealmakers
appear in the night

The Driskill
leather and Longhorns
  set the stage for historic
wheeling and dealing

Dirty Sixth
cops block off the streets
  but the noise and partiers
exceed their limits

Waterloo Records
grooves from wall to wall
  music addicts might just have
met their Waterloo

PSA
quiet while watching
  or else you'll get taken out
Tarantino-style

Seaholm Power Plant
Art Deco delight
    shines after development
a sign of the times

Patience
anticipation
Congress Ave, watchers and bats

Unlimited
our skyline stretches
 as Austin ambition grows
reach exceeding grasp

Pennybacker Bridge
happy blue above
    double rainbow of amber
happy blue below

Allen's Boots
tourists and Texans
  linger over stitched leather
  seeking their solemates

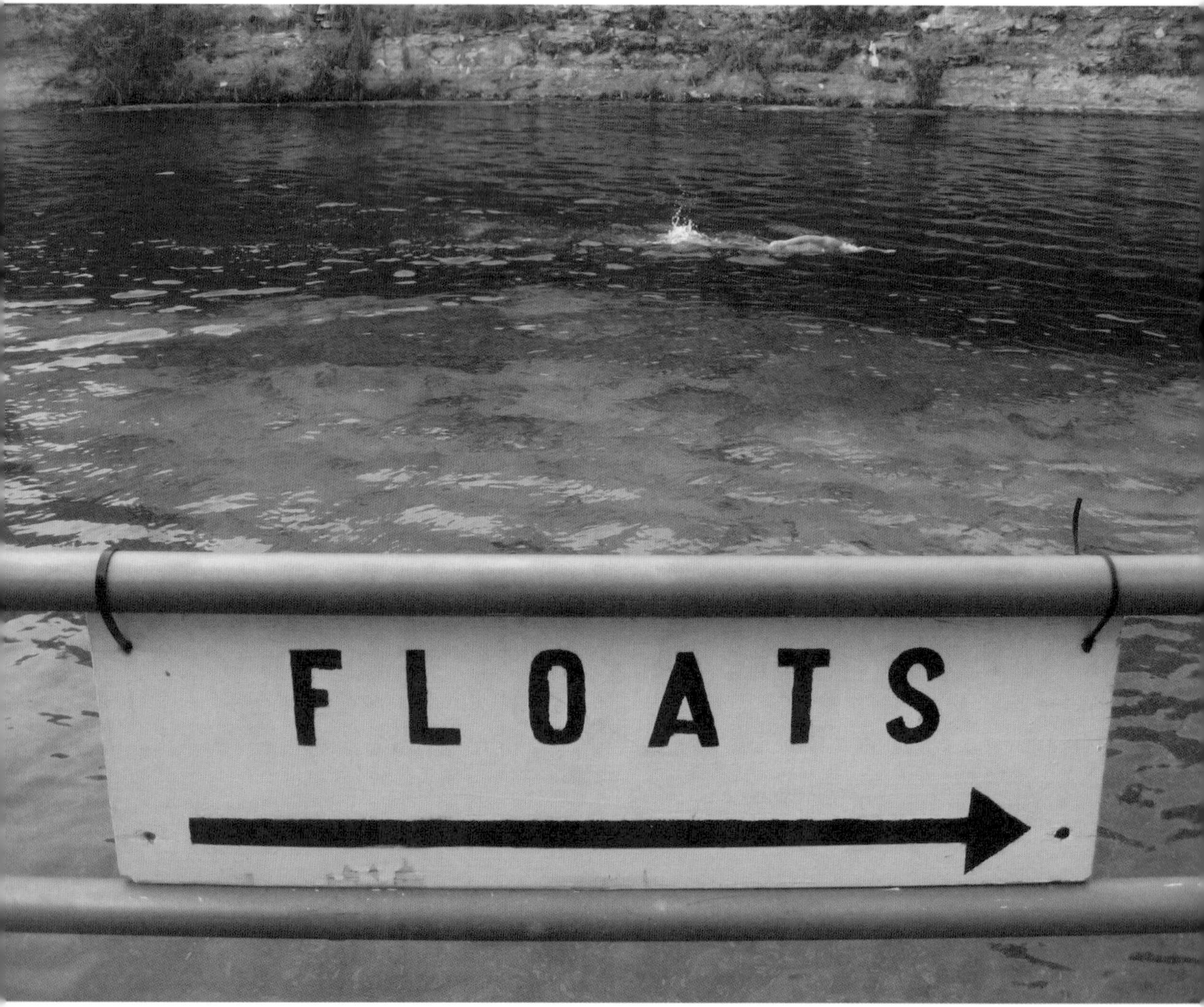
FLOATS

Hidden

nudists, tattoos, kids
  lots to see at Barton Springs
but: salamanders?

Barton Springs

68 degrees
  spring water keeps it perfect
let's go and chill out

Nippy

topless sunbather
  exits Barton Springs; it's clear
the water is cold

Eventful Austin

filled with food and song
Austin weekends overflow
like the parking lots

If you like it, Austin probably has a festival for it. Because this city
doesn't just celebrate good music and fabulous food and drink.
In fact, we've got festivals dedicated to quilts, comics, books, kites,
motorcycles, puns, custom cars and sad donkeys. Yep. True story.

Trail of Lights
wait your turn to walk
  sparkling scenes and fussy kids
on brilliant display

Rodeo Style
believe it or not
  some Texans wear boots and hats
for work, not just fun

Rodeo Austin
our own rodeo
draws real, ropin' cowboys and
folks just dressed that way

ACL Fest
crowds stream through Zilker
    the air thickens with music
among other things

ACL wristband
   delivers dozens of bands
and two aching feet

Pecan Street Festival
day drinking on Sixth
  booths crowded with arts and crap
turkey legs beckon

ACL Quest
I heard the best bands
    as I wandered through tattoos
searching for our flag

Republic of Texas Biker Rally
leathered guys and dolls
some gangsters, some retirees
roaring bravado

Statesman Cap10K
finish line fashion:
    tutus, wigs, Fat Elvis suits
quite the fab runway

Fun Fun Fun Fest
a naming challenge:
    what to call a music fest
that's three times the fun?

Blues on the Green
pray for summer rain
   lest drought and dust turn the show
to blues on the brown

Formula One
rich Europeans
   bring Austinites a taste of
life in the fast lane

Scorcher
August inferno
   perfect time of year for that
hot sauce festival

Carnaval
one night in Brazil
   too much flirting, fun and flesh
call the Samba cops

Zilker Kite Festival
let's go fly a kite
windy weekend at Zilker
trees stretch to snag one

UT Austin

no mere college town
at the heart of this city
it's Longhorn Nation

Like most things Texan, the University of Texas flagship school is big,
bold and unabashedly proud. The school spirit of students, alumni and fans
is contagious -- and always on full display, from the distinctive burnt
orange gear to the rampant flashing of the "Hook 'Em" sign. Go 'Horns!

On Guadalupe
see, hear and feel it
  for UT kids the Drag is
anything but a

Sign Language
five-fingered salute
   means "Hook 'em Horns!" (or "Loser"
if you're an Aggie)

UT Football
fall comes to Austin
    everything but the trees
turns to burnt orange

For the Record
Mack Brown's legacy:
  a brighter football future
plus a rosy past

Beware
don't cheer for OU
  because the eyes of Texas
are upon U

Red River Showdown
sure, pride is at stake
  but more important than that
a big golden hat

Spirited
each time UT wins
   in Austin and far beyond
Longhorns get lit, too

Workload
so much to study!
   pulling all-nighter to plan
ACL Fest picks

Go 'Horns
let's light the tower!
  bold display designed to match
the fans' inner glow

Bevo
more than a mascot
  this longhorn is each Longhorn's
spirit animal

Conundrum
haiku for UT
  ignites syllabic debate
burnt orange? burnt or-ange?

Lone Stars
spirit of Texans
  burns not just bright but also
deep in the heart of

Texas Exes
few things are prouder
   than a Longhorn - except for
a former Longhorn

Tailgate
parking lot party
   Longhorns grill, guzzle and gab
you can't beat this spread

Austin Outdoors

Austin insiders
love it even more when they're
being outsiders

The River City is rich with vibrant outdoor spaces, and blessed
with the kind of weather that invites you out to swim and bike and
boat and picnic pretty much year-round. In Austin, you spend
a good amount of time in the great outdoors. Hey, it's only natural.

Photo Op
Austin fields in Spring
  bouquets of families pick
bluebonnet poses

Mountain Laurel
heavy with purple
 dizzying Grape Kool-Aid buzz
Spring leaves us punch drunk

Standing By
out-of-towners look
  at paddlers on the lake
and ask friends, "What's SUP?"

Lake Travis
wake boarders catch air
  lake babes catch rays on the deck
summer showing off

Hippie Hollow
dare to bare it all
  where clothing is optional
but sunscreen is not

Lake Life
kick back in a cove
  all you need: a cooler and
a friend with a boat

Heavenly
Barton Creek greenbelt
  crowds flock on summer Sundays
to worship outdoors

Zilker Park
balls, kites, frisbees, dogs
  unleashed upon the great field
weekend free-for-all

Town Lake Trail
in Austin some find
   that they can follow their bliss
on the beaten path

Deep Eddy Pool
cold as Barton Springs
    more families than hipsters
so -- not quite as cool?

Deep Eddy

sparkling spring-fed pool
   crystal clear and cold all year
swimmers lap it up

Veloway

wheels-only trailway
   keeps Austin's street pedalers
ahead of the curve

Lady Bird Johnson Wildflower Center
refuge for natives
  honors the First Lady's wish
to keep Austin wild

New Year's Polar Bear Plunge
cold springs cleanse our souls
  wash away regrets, shock us
into new resolve

Austin Music

booming through bar doors
this Live Music Capital
makes tourists take note

Street corners. Grocery stores. Schools. Pools. It's hard to
find a place where someone *isn't* playing music in our fair city,
deservedly dubbed the "Live Music Capital of the World."
Country to conjunto, reggae to rock, you can hear it all, all week
long, all over town. In Austin, there's always music in your ears --
and a song in your heart.

Saxon Pub
Monday night line-up
   funk, blues, country, pop, rap, jazz
and that's just Bob S.

ACL Live
the best live music
   in the whole country is here
within city limits

Oil Can Harry's
when dance fever strikes
   head straight here – guaranteed to
have a gay old time

Janis
early Austin scene
   gave us a life and music
ended all too soon

Labeled
from Butthole Surfers
   to Spoon and White Ghost Shivers
Austin band names rock

Willie

red headed stranger
  funny how time slips away
still crazy for you

Broken Spoke
locals scoot their boots
   across wood, two-stepping past
tourists' two left feet

Dale Watson
drawlin', truck-drivin'
   troubadour sings of a love
as deep as his voice

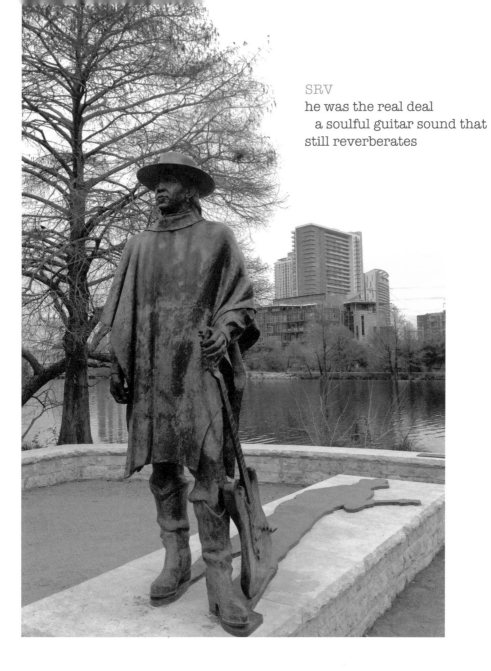

SRV

he was the real deal
  a soulful guitar sound that
still reverberates

In Sync

deejay starts his jam
  bass and lasers pulse as he
takes us for a spin

Deal
five-dollar cover
    gets you legendary blues,
your fill of heartache

Noteworthy
South Congress classic
    just a little honky-tonk
where big names were made

GARY
CLARK, JR
MARCH 14, 2012

Homeboy
when you've done so well
   singing the blues, it might get
hard to sing the blues

Austin Eats & Drinks

homestyle meets high-end
five-star dining in flip flops
our appetites grow

Hungry in Austin? Lucky you. We've got as many types of food
as we have music. Once known for Tex-Mex and margaritas,
we've now got gourmet food trucks and craft brews galore.
Of course, we all still appreciate a homemade tamale
washed down with a frosty Lone Star every now and then.

Amy's
scoop slap smash pound plop
  servers smoosh sweets into cream
go flippin' crazy

Hyde Park Bar & Grill
ah, you chose wisely
  seeking the best fries, you found
that fork in the road

Hey Cupcake!
when dessert is served
   from an old Airstream, that's just
icing on the cake

Salvation
breakfast miracle
    virtue wrapped in flour or corn
hangovers vanish

Queso
pool of gooey gold
  naked chips in hand, we pause
who'll take the first dip?

Hudson's on the Bend
wild beasts for dinner
  let's all make the trip out west
if anyone's game

The Oasis
proof in each sunset
  the best thing 'bout eating here
ain't on the menu

Gastropub
such bespoke flavors
  the plates keep getting smaller
the prices, bigger

Free Lunch
snack on smorgasboard
  of Central Market samples
(we all do it, right?)

Magnolia Cafe
pancakes and tacos
  best wee hours munchies, unless
you count Kerbey Lane

Kerbey Lane
gingerbread pancakes
  the best breakfast this side of
Magnolia Cafe

Threadgill's
everything's home-cooked
Texas-style, like the music
now that's comfort food

Farmers' Market
farm-fresh and full-color
  just-picked goodness nourishes
my Instagram feed

Marketing
we didn't invent
  breakfast tacos; we simply
sell them like we did

Uchi
elegant morsels
  leave us thinking we live in
Tokyo, Texas

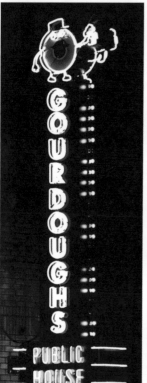

Margaritas
avocado? sure!
   any flavor goes, here in
Margaritaville

Artisanal
handcrafted cocktails
   millennials' Manhattans
not so old-fashioned

Beer Me
craft brew connoisseurs
   are in heaven, but sometimes
a Shiner's fine, too

Rainey Street
old and decrepit
   homes turned into bars for the
young and beautiful

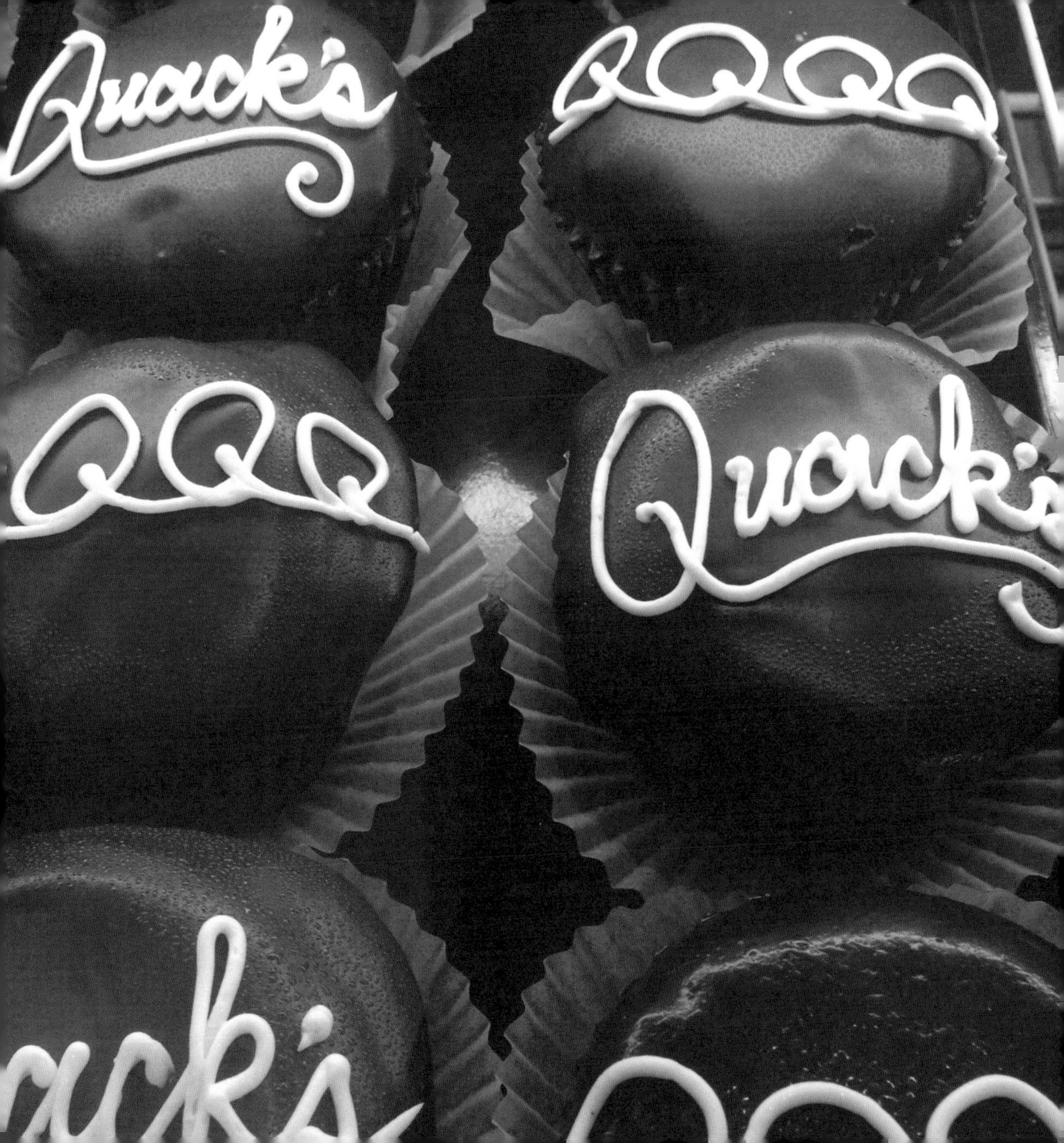
Quack's

Shhh
BBQ secret:
    the best way to get the best
just move to Austin

                                        Stubbs
                                        ribs, brisket, sausage
                                            served smokin' with their sauce and
                                        a side of music

Franklin BBQ
must-eat BBQ
    it takes hours to get it right
and just to get it

Austinites

living in Austin
reminds you it's cool to be
living in Austin

Coders and cowboys. Artists and activists. Professors and politicians. Some are from here; a lot are not. There's one thing, though, that this eclectic bunch shares: a passion for the place we call home. And yeah, we sometimes like to talk about how awesome it is. But can you blame us, really?

Ann Richards
white-haired queen of quips
   no beating around the Bush
profane and profound

Lady Bird Johnson
First Lady's vision
   so green and ever-growing
spread like wildflowers

Lance Armstrong
race to the finish
   despite that yellow jersey
scandal catches up

Matthew McConaughey
dazed and confused star
   marches to the beat of a
different bongo

Michael Dell
UT student geek
   turned computer parts to gold
that's quite a start-up

Richard Linklater
boyhood filmmaker
   grown to Oscar nominee
hardly a slacker

Hipster
are you wearing that
retro thing for real or
ironically?

Barbara Jordan
her constitution
    strong, brave, purposeful - and made
for defending ours

Covered

frat boys stroll down Sixth
  bouncers yell, "No cover charge!"
music to their ears

Hair Today

wear beards, dreads, man buns
  style it any way you like
but come on, mullets?

Fashion

love the skinny jeans
  lookin' good with your plaid shirt
woot! that fanny pack!

Drivers

Minis and pickups
  coexist (surprisingly)
on I-35

The Game
shouting and screaming
  tried and true high school drama
must end in heartbreak

Tatted
Austin loves its ink
  going sleeveless, sans tattoos
makes you a rebel

Keeping Austin Weird

a new conundrum:
how to foster the funky
when weird is normal

In Austin, we celebrate the offbeat, the eccentric, the crazy and
the creative. And many of us strive to keep the conventional and
the corporate at bay. Our quirkiness is deeply rooted, though, so no
matter how Austin changes, weird will always be welcome here.

O. Henry Pun-Off World Championship

punslingers gather
  and jest for a wordy cause
they serve home-groan jokes

Eeyore's Birthday Party

come for drum circles
  to cheer that depressed donkey
wear your birthday suit

Evening Line Up
the pedicabbers
  ride and wait and ride and wait
an endless cycle

Segway Tours
as they roll down Sixth
  I want to tell the tourists,
"That's a nice Segway."

Cathedral of Junk
classic south Austin
  making fun from the funky
trash turned to treasure

Ginny's Little Longhorn Saloon
squeeze in on Sunday
  you could really clean up at
chicken shit bingo

Street Art
words into pictures
   artists vandalize the bland
litter with color

Peter Pan Putt-Putt
towering T.rex
    are you another Austin
endangered species?

What the Flock
right off 360
   drivers become birdwatchers
can't stop thinking pink

Wheels
Teslas to Vespas
  street style ranges high to low
whatever moves you

i love you
so much

Jo's Coffee
how I adore you
   tall, dark and so very hot
(my coffee, that is)

78704
laid back, funky, weird
  no matter what you call us
you've got our number

Love to Hate

capital of cool
everyone loves Austin
except when they don't

Yes, Austin's wonderful. But it's not perfect, and it seems we all like to
gripe about something, from the highway traffic to the hipsters.
As with every love/hate relationship, though, we're willing to take the bad
with the good. Because there's far more of the latter than the former.

Cedar Fever
great clouds of pollen
  come from junipers mating
tree sex makes us sneeze

Achoo
allergy season
  worst time of year, best excuse
for not doing things

Uncool
summer in Texas
  triple-digit temps blasting
all over Facebook

Brrr
middle of August
  temps drop to the mid-90s
that's quite a cold front

Boom
you moved to Austin!
   good for you, but now it's hard
for Austin to move

Grackles
black blots against sky
  raucous cackles threaten like
that Hitchcock movie

Locals
say "SouthBySouthWest"
  "Not from around here, are you?"
(we call it "SouthBy")

That Time of Year
when hipsters invade
  a town chock full o' hipsters
it's SXSW

Pflugerville

Pflugerville is Pfun!
  they're Pfriendly Pfolks; but Austin
just says, "What the Pf?"

Huh?

"Man-shack"? "Man-chaw-kah"?
  here, pronunciation's hard
except for: "Aus-tin"

Hipster Kids

mini skinny jeans
  kale juice in their sippy cups
cooler hats than yours

Mobility
look at the bright side
   sitting in downtown traffic
makes texting easy

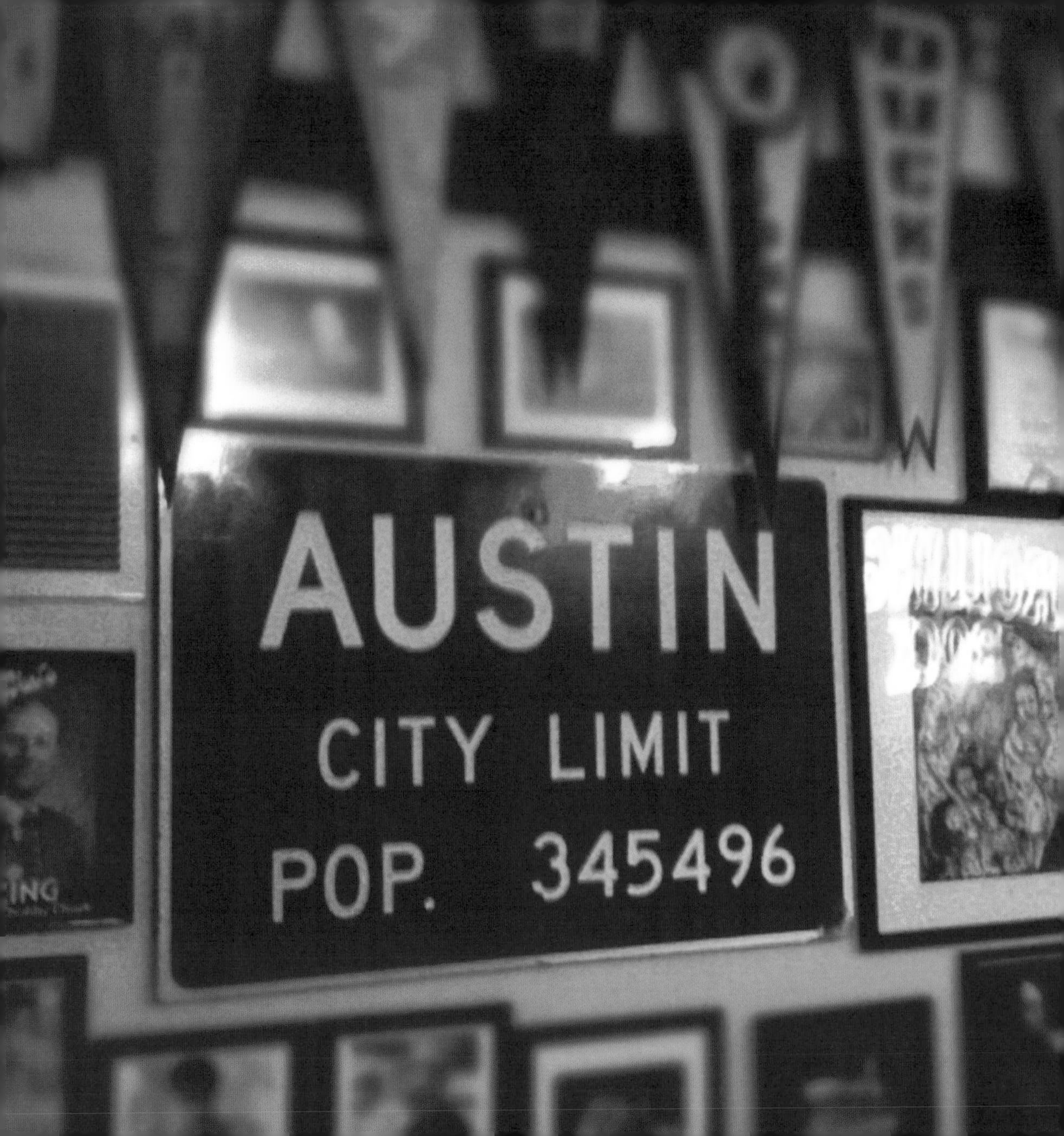
AUSTIN
CITY LIMIT
POP. 345496

Lost Austin

old makes way for new
we push on while looking back
keeping weird at heart

Sure, change happens. And with it come fresh places and
people to get to know and love. But just for a moment,
let's wax nostalgic and pay tribute to some old Austin favorites.
They may no longer be with us, but they'll never be forgotten.

Leslie
he ran for mayor
  just a thonged guy trying to
make a few things right

Fresh Start
Whole Foods, the '90s:
  nut butters and tattooed clerks
before they were cool

Dallas Night Club
ladies' night at last
  parking lot packed with pickups
plenty more inside

Aquafest
down by the river
  Dolly sang and drag boats sped
till all went under

Austin Past
once upon a time
  it filled the streets of Austin
we miss free parking

Liberty Lunch
cold beer and hot bands
  big sound under big sky - then
the dive took a dive

Spamarama
a fest of canned meat
  we ate Spamcakes, Spam sundaes
and then tossed our Spam

Old Timers
The Armadillo,
  Aquafest, Liberty Lunch...
Austin, before you

Katz's Deli
craving a Rueben
    so of course I'm wishing that
Katz's Never Klosed

Las Manitas
missing those migas
    menudo and chorizo
ah, Lost Manitas!

Pecan Grove RV Park
Airstreams and campers
  a village of vintage junk
till the condos come

RunTex
haven for runners
  until the last customer
crossed the finish line

37th Street
Christmas lights gone wild
  and that feeling in the air?
electricity

HAIKUDOS

First of all, a great big group hug and shout out to all my Kickstarter backers. Thank you so much for your generosity and faith in me.

Secondly, thanks to all these wonderful people, in Austin and beyond:

Kate and Ella, for helping me see our city through youthful eyes, and for tolerating my constant picture-taking.

Anne, for your undying enthusiasm, patience, creativity, and sense of humor.

Katrina, for your sisterhood and support.

Becka, for being a fellow Austinphile and poetry geek, and for your wise counsel.

Donald, Ron and Ralph, for your feedback and encouragement.

Terry, for being my publishing Sherpa.

Tony and The Writers' League of Texas, for your professional support.

Bob Schneider, Owen Egerton, Sara Hickman and Wally Williams, for your way with words.

Corey, Rocky and Deborah, for your generosity.

My Wednesday morning friends, for your weekly shot of wisdom and love.

Paul, for encouraging and inspiring my love for Austin from the beginning.

Brockoli and Stork, for your friendship and your confidence in me.

KJ, Mary, Diane, Susan, Renee, MaryEllen and BK, for believing in me.

My mom and dad, for the creative DNA.

CARLOTTA EIKE STANKIEWICZ
is a writer, wanderer, poet and picture-taker.
She's loved Austin since she moved here in 1992.
Haiku Austin is her first book.
You can find more of her poetry and photography at
haikuAustin.com and wellversedmom.com.